AF228833

Angelfish live in
the sea.

5

Angelfish are colorful.

This angelfish is
blue and yellow.

This angelfish is orange and white.

Some angelfish
are small.

13

Some angelfish
are big.

15

Angelfish swim.

17

Angelfish eat.

19

This angelfish is hiding!

21

This is a queen angelfish.

23

Published in 2026 by The Rosen Publishing Group, Inc.
2544 Clinton Street, Buffalo, NY 14224

First Edition

Editor: Theresa Emminizer
Book Design: Jeffrey Taylor

Photo Credits: Cover Jan Leya/Shutterstock.com; p. 3 Ricardo_Dias/Shutterstock.com; p. 5 glebantiy/Shutterstock.com; p. 7 chonlasub woravichan/Shutterstock.com; p. 9 Daryl Duda/Shutterstock.com; p. 11 Vojce/Shutterstock.com; p. 13 KITTIPONG SOMKLANG/Shutterstock.com; p. 15 jwscuba/Shutterstock.com; p. 17 Damsea/Shutterstock.com; p. 19 thomas eder/Shutterstock.com; p. 21 Thierry Eldenweil/Shutterstock.com; p. 23 Galina Savina/Shutterstock.com.

Cataloging-in-Publication Data

Names: Emminizer, Theresa.
Title: Angelfish / Theresa Emminizer.
Description: Buffalo, New York : PowerKids Press, 2026. | Series: Superstars of the sea Identifiers: ISBN 9781499451405 (pbk.) | ISBN 9781499451412 (library bound) | ISBN 9781499451429 (ebook)
Subjects: LCSH: Marine angelfishes--Juvenile literature.
Classification: LCC QL638.P768 E46 2026 | DDC 597.'72--dc23

Manufactured in the United States of America

Some of the images in this book illustrate individuals who are models. The depictions do not imply actual situations or events.

CPSIA Compliance Information: Batch #CSPK26. For further information contact Rosen Publishing at 1-800-237-9932.

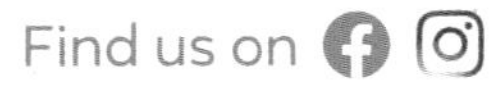